RISING STARS

HOMEWORK ACTIVITIES

Science Level 2

Louise Moore

Contents

How to use *Rising Stars Homework Activities Science*

Rising Stars Homework Activities Science is an updated series of photocopiable activities offering a ready-made solution for homework or classwork. They have been written so that no preparation is required – simply photocopy and go! The activities can be used alongside all your other teaching resources and are ideal for homework or extra practice in class.

This book consists of:

- a warm-up activity for the level pupils should already be working at;
- activities for different topics at the new higher level;
- a final check-up activity for the level pupils have been working towards;
- answers for all the activities.

The warm-up activity (Activity A)

If pupils score over 80% on the initial activity they are ready to start working from the book. If they score lower they need more work on the previous level.

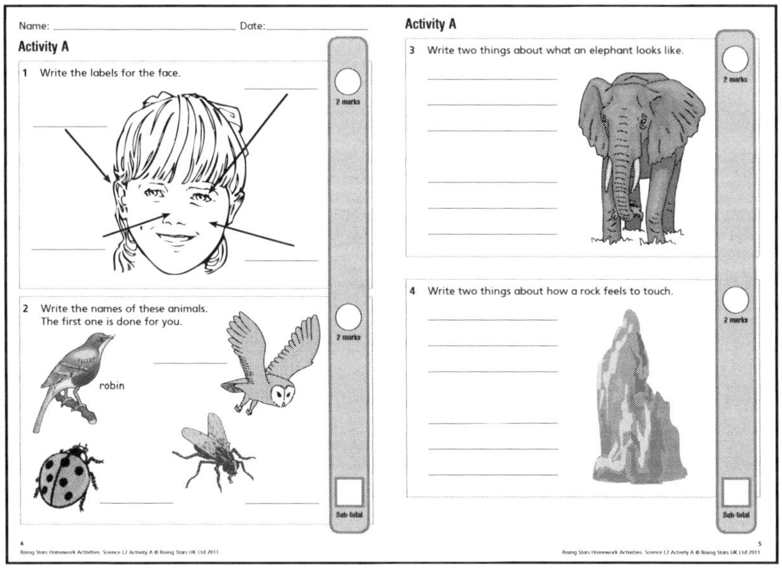

Topic activities

Use these activities before and after studying a topic to identify strengths and weaknesses. You can be confident that pupils who achieve 80% or more for any activity are working at the target level in that topic.

A self-assessment grid at the end of each topic allows you to complete a traffic light symbol showing how well the topic was understood. In addition, pupils can write an 'I CAN' statement in the space provided.

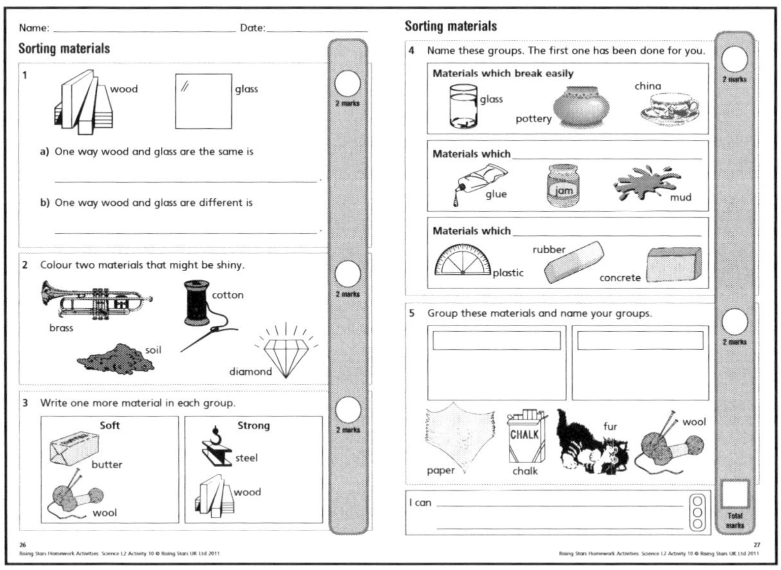

Answers are provided at the end of the book.

The check-up activity (Activity B)

This is a summative activity at the level pupils should have attained by the end of the book.

If pupils achieve over 80% they are ready to move to the next book. If they score lower they need more practice on the current level.

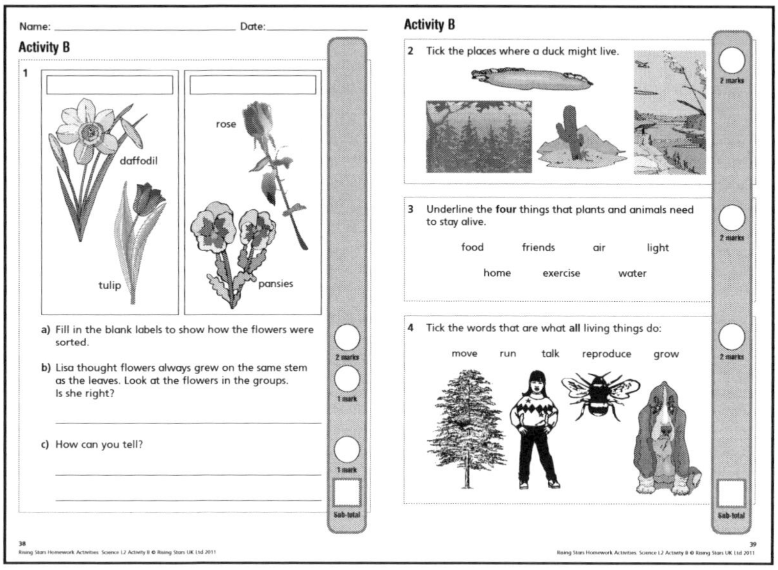
Name: Date:

Activity B

1

rose

daffodil

tulip

pansies

a) Fill in the blank labels to show how the flowers were sorted.

2 marks

b) Lisa thought flowers always grew on the same stem as the leaves. Look at the flowers in the groups. Is she right?

1 mark

c) How can you tell?

1 mark

Sub-total

Activity B

2 Tick the places where a duck might live.

2 marks

3 Underline the **four** things that plants and animals need to stay alive.

food friends air light

home exercise water

2 marks

4 Tick the words that are what **all** living things do:

move run talk reproduce grow

2 marks

Sub-total

Additional notes

This book has a good proportion of questions where children have to express ideas and concepts in their own words or show how they have arrived at an answer. This means that the activities can be used as diagnostic tools that will allow you to spot and correct any misconceptions linked with a particular topic at an early stage in a pupil's learning process. In addition, some questions have multiple answers or require a pupil's interpretation of the information. At least one sample answer is given, but you should use your professional judgement when assessing pupil answers to these questions.

Help with reading is allowed, especially for younger pupils, in all the books.

Name: ______________________ Date: ______________

Activity A

1 Write the labels for the face.

2 marks

2 Write the names of these animals.
The first one is done for you.

robin

2 marks

Sub-total

Activity A

3 Write two things about what an elephant looks like.

2 marks

4 Write two things about how a rock feels to touch.

2 marks

Sub-total

Activity A

5 What will happen when the switch is put on?

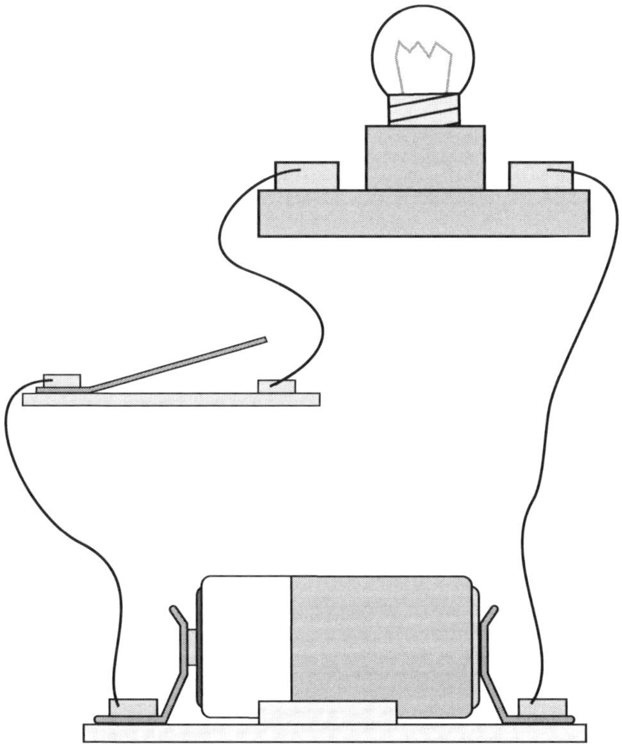

1 mark

6 What will happen when a handle is pulled?

1 mark

Sub-total

Activity A

7 **a)** Colour the sources of light.

b) Write the names underneath the pictures you have coloured.

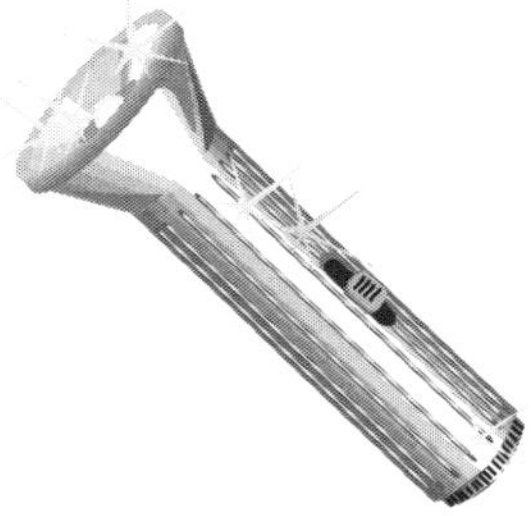

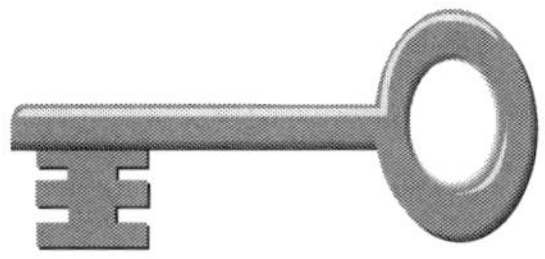

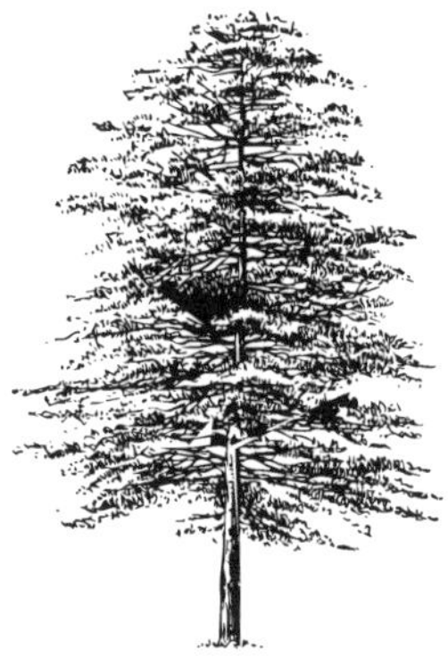

4 marks

8 How can Billy make the car move?

____

____

____

____

1 mark

Total marks

Name: ______________________ Date: ______________

Collecting data

1 John thinks ants prefer damp places. He puts some ants in a tray with wet soil at one side and dry soil at the other.

a) Circle the side of the tray John thinks the ants will go to.

b) What should John do with the ants when he finishes his test?

____

____

____

____

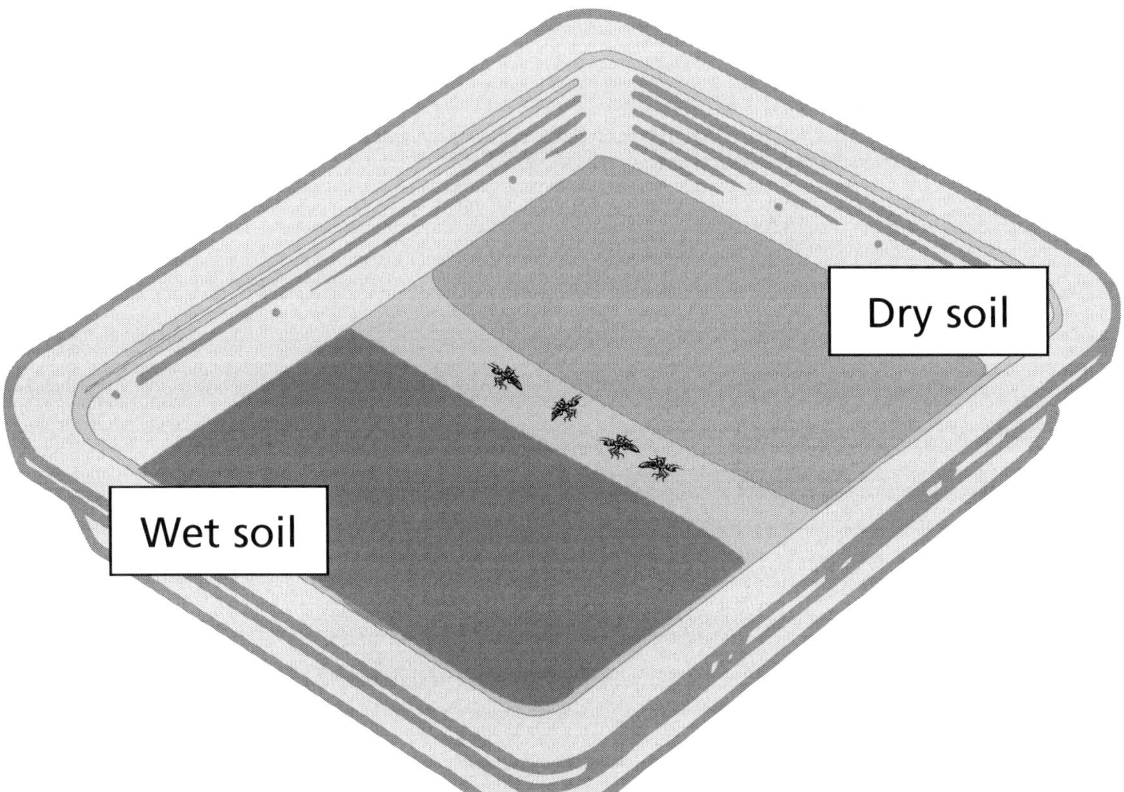

2 marks

Collecting data

2 Anna is finding out about how people grow.
Finish filling in her chart for Callum and Jill.
One answer has been done for you.

	Child's name
a) taller	
b) longer legs	
longer arms	*Callum*
c) bigger hands	

3 marks

3 Nazir and Amy want to know if their pet rabbits prefer carrots or lettuce.
Nazir says he will give them carrots one day and lettuce the next, to see which they eat fastest.
Amy says she will give them carrots and lettuce together and see which they eat most of.

a) Who has the best plan? ______________________

1 mark

b) Why? ______________________

____

2 marks

c) How could they find out if their rabbits preferred water or milk to drink?

____

____

2 marks

I can ______________________

____

Total marks

Name: ______________________ Date: ______________

Interpreting results

1 Mary thinks all lights need electricity to work. Sam shows her a collection of light sources.

a) Was Mary right? ______________________

b) How can you tell? ______________________

____

____

2 marks

2 Cal makes a table to show where he found animals in the playground.

Under a stone	In the flowerbed	In the wall	On the tree
slug woodlice snail	snail butterfly worm ladybird	ants spider	snail beetle ladybird caterpillar

a) How many different kinds of animals did he find in the flowerbed? ______________

b) Where did he find a ladybird?

______________ and ______________ .

2 marks

Interpreting results

2 c) How many places did he find a snail? ______________

d) Where was the darkest place he looked?

____

e) How many different kinds of animals did he find altogether? ___________

3 marks

3 Josh makes the loudest sound he can on some instruments. He puts the instruments in order from the softest sound to the loudest sound.

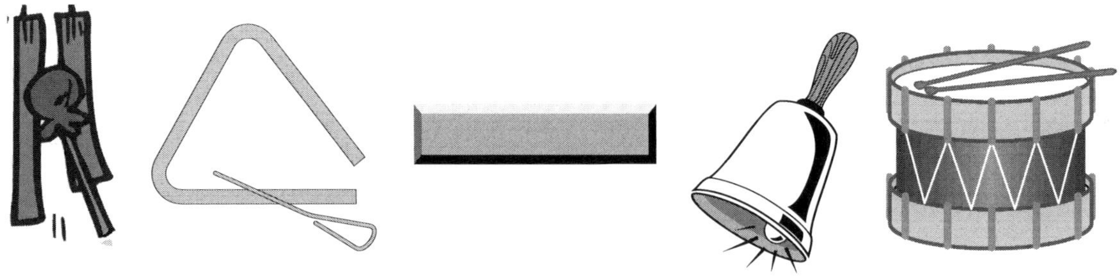

Softest | Loudest

a) Circle the instrument(s) that make a louder sound than the wood block.

b) Josh says that he made louder sounds with the metal instruments than with the others. Colour the instrument that shows he is wrong.

c) Does the bell make a softer sound than the triangle?

____

3 marks

I can ____

____

Total marks

Name: ______________________________ Date: ________________

Living things

1

a) Circle the living things.

b) Tick the things that will grow.

4 marks

2

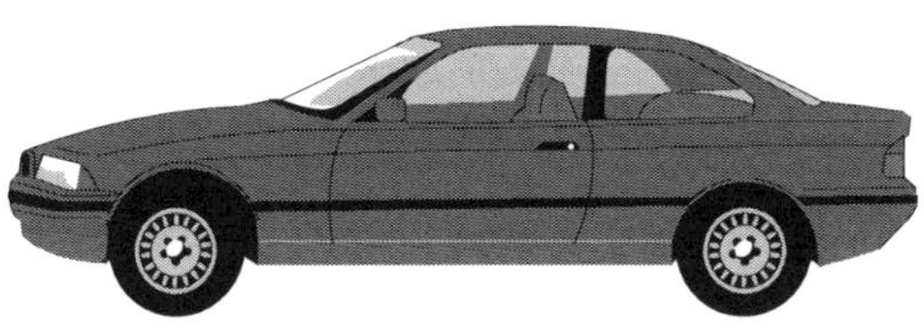

a) Circle the living things that can make themselves move.

b) Tick the living things that use their senses.

4 marks

Living things

3 Draw something else on the picture that a rabbit needs to stay alive.

1 mark

4 Tick two things a dog needs to stay alive.

1 mark

I can ______________________________

____

Total marks

Name: ______________________ Date: ______________

Grouping living things

1 Draw and label two more animals in each group.

2 marks

No legs	**Four legs**
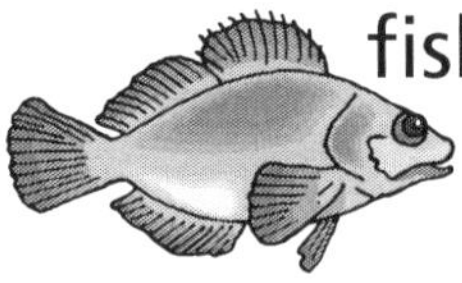 fish  slug	 cat 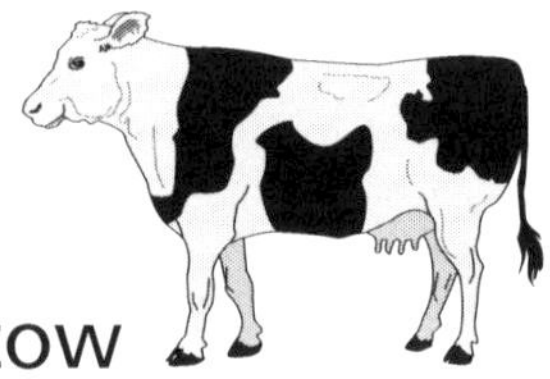 cow
____________ ____________	____________ ____________

2 Fill in the name for these groups of plants.

2 marks

____________	____________

Grouping living things

3 Match these animals to the right group by drawing lines.

Animals that can fly	Animals that can't fly

2 marks

4 Draw and label one more plant in each group.

Plants you can eat

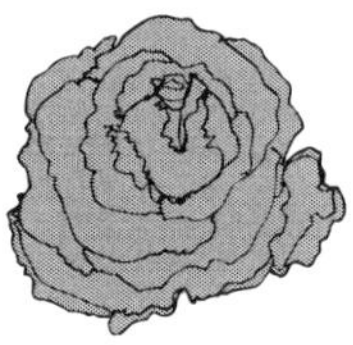

lettuce

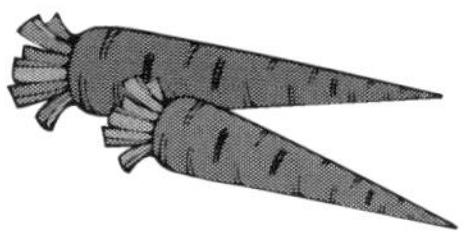

carrots

Plants you can't eat

holly berries

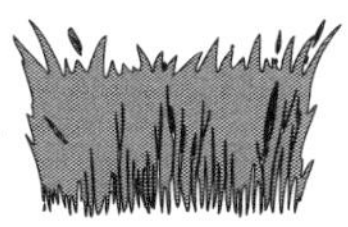

grass

2 marks

5 Group these animals and name each group.

crocodile

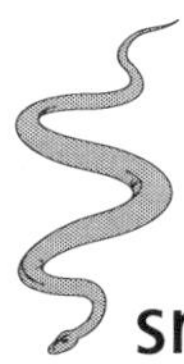

snake

rabbit

fish

horse

2 marks

I can ______________________________

____

Total marks

Name: ______________________ Date: ______________

Plants

1 **a)** Write one way Mira can tell that her plant has grown the most.

1 mark

____

b) Tick three things Mira's plant needs to stay alive.

2 marks

light ☐

night-time ☐

water ☐

pot ☐

warmth ☐

2 Fill in the labels correctly. The first one is done for you.

2 marks

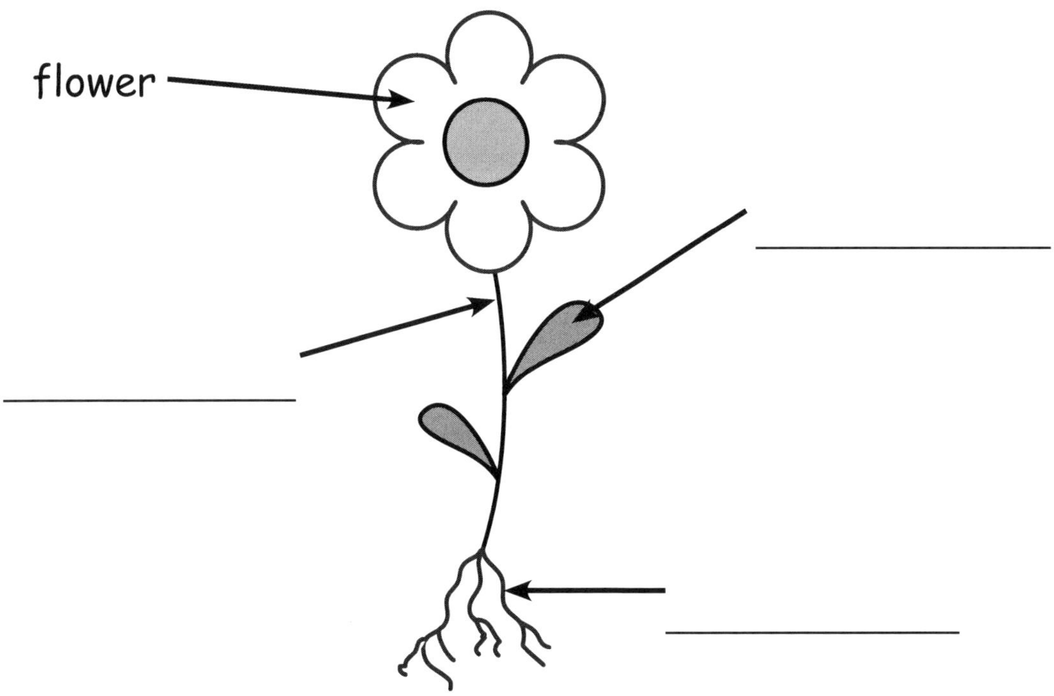

Plants

3 Fill in the names of the plants.

dandelion daisy daffodil buttercup

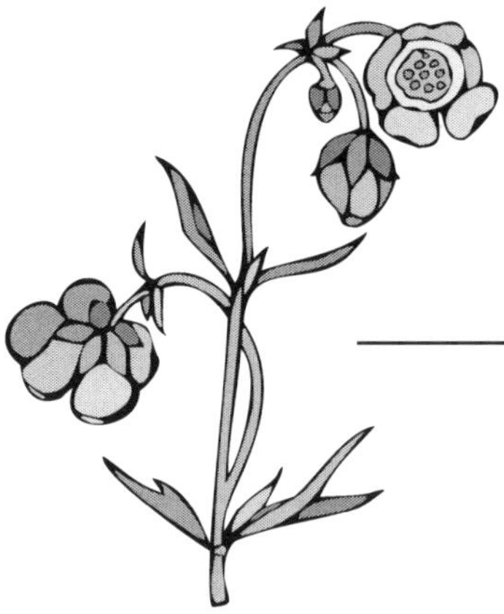

2 marks

4 Write two things we use plants for.

2 marks

5 Dan ate an apple. He kept the seeds and planted them. What will grow?

1 mark

I can

Total marks

Name: ______________________ Date: ______________

Animals

1 Match the animals to their young.

1 mark

2 Label the parts of the animals.

4 marks

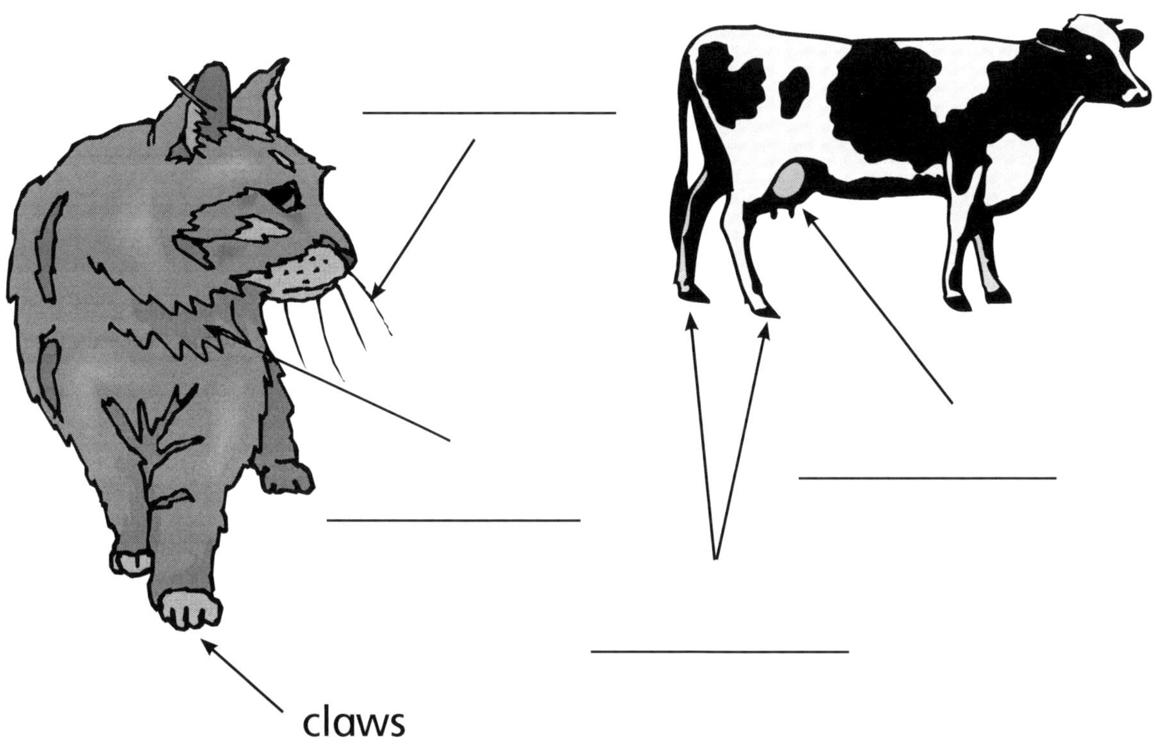

Animals

3 Circle all the animals.

2 marks

4 Tom saw a tadpole. What will it change into?

____

1 mark

5 Circle the things that all animals need to survive.

home   water   friends   food   clothes

2 marks

6 Write the names of these animals.

_______________ _______________ _______________ _______________

2 marks

I can ____

____

Total marks

Name: ______________________________ Date: ________________

Habitats

1 Join the living things to the place where they live.

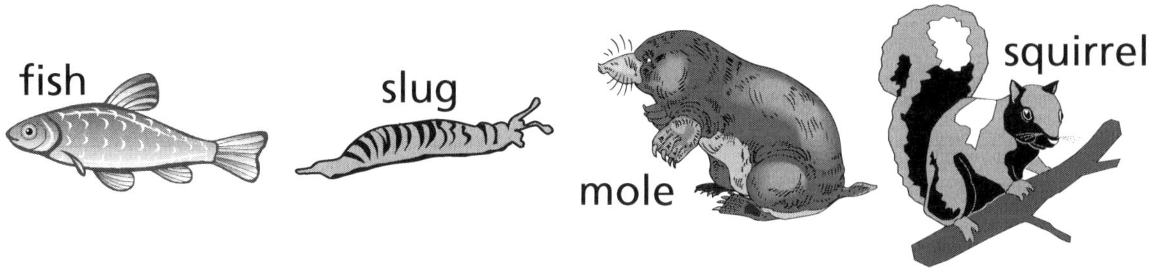

in the soil | pond | in a tree | under a rock

2 marks

2 In the picture, put a X in two places where a slug might live.

2 marks

Habitats

3 a) Name two things that might live in a pond.

______________________ ______________________

4 marks

b) Name two things that might live in a tree.

______________________ ______________________

4 Give two differences between these two places where animals might live.

2 marks

Beach

Forest

____

____

____

____

I can ____

____

Total marks

Name: ______________________ Date: ______________

Humans

1 Fill in the labels for the parts of the body.

2 marks

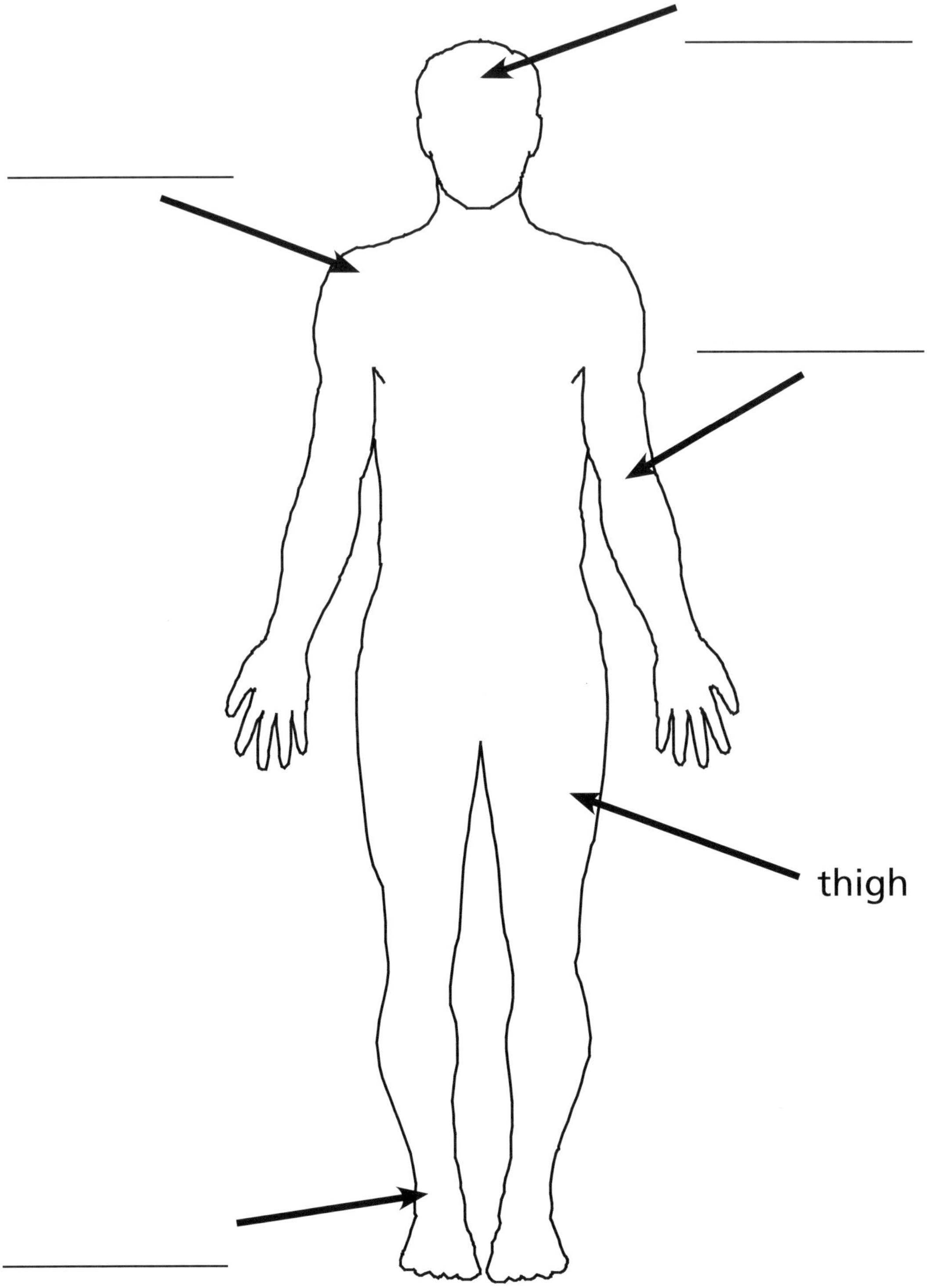

Humans

2 **a)** Give two ways all people are alike.

____

____

2 marks

b) Give one way people are different.

____

1 mark

3 Write one thing you can't change about the way you look.

____

1 mark

4 Write one way your body will have changed by next year.

____

1 mark

5 How can medicines be dangerous?

____

1 mark

6 Jane runs across the playground. Write two words to describe how her body feels afterwards.

___________________________ ___________________________

2 marks

I can ____

____

Total marks

Name: ______________________________ Date: ________________

Properties of materials

1 Colour the manmade materials.

wood

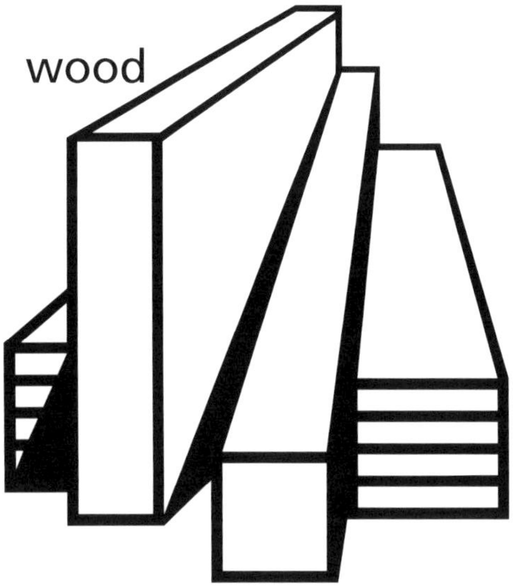

brick

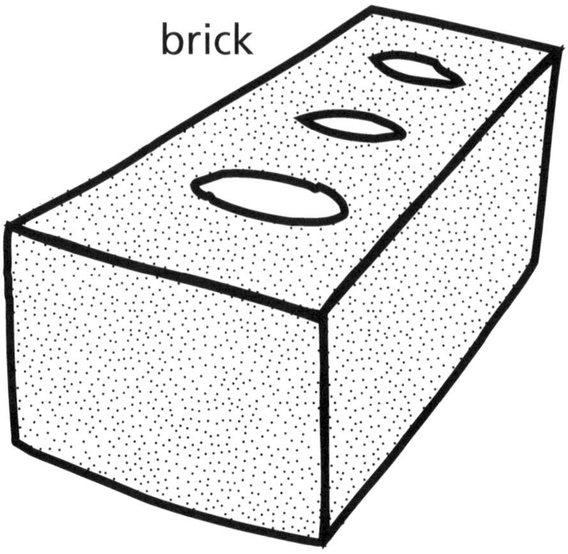

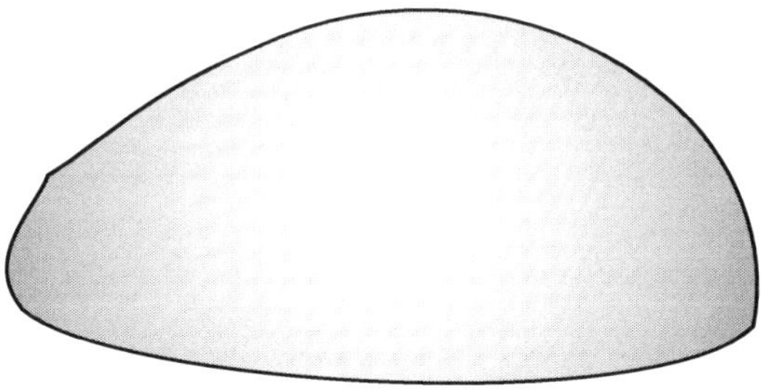

stone

plastic

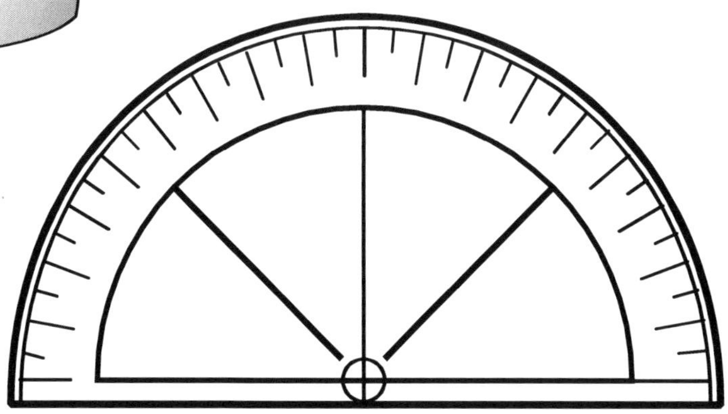

2 marks

2 **a)** You could make a table from ____________________ .

b) You could make a coat from ____________________ .

2 marks

Properties of materials

3 Colour the materials that are waterproof.

plastic

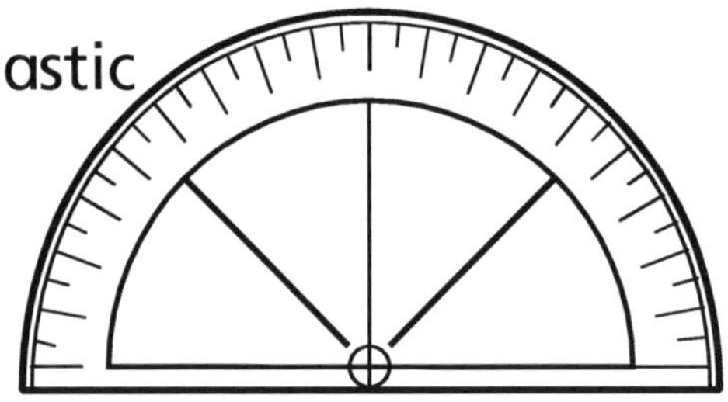

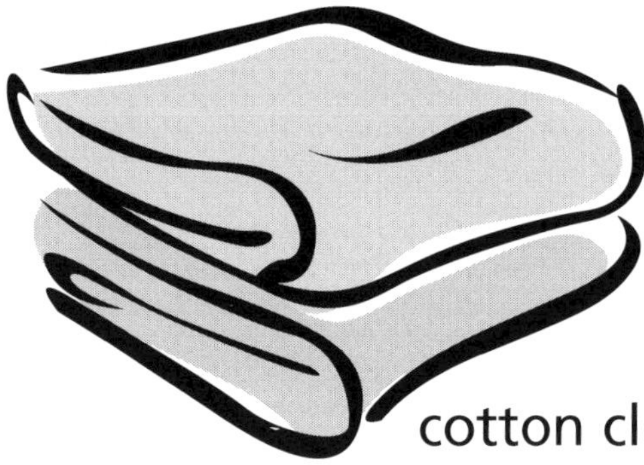

cotton cloth

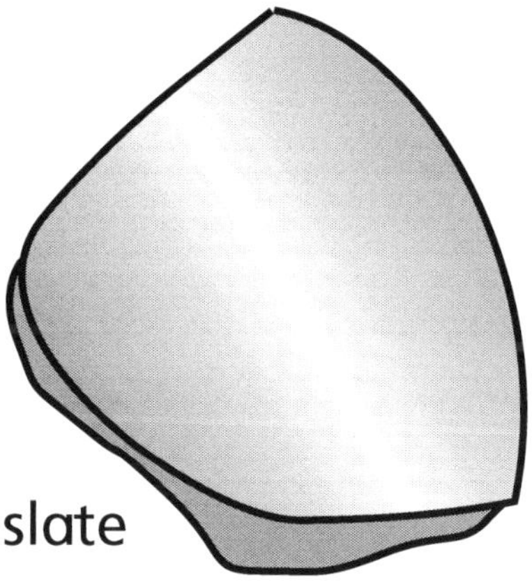

slate

sponge

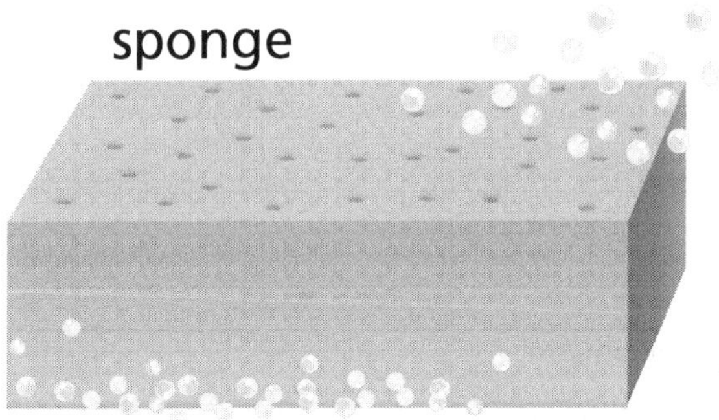

2 marks

4 Match each material on the left to a property on the right. You can only use each word once.

glass	strong
wood	transparent
rubber	warm
wool	bendy

2 marks

5 Two things you could make from metal are

____________________ and ____________________ .

2 marks

I can ____

____

Total marks

Name: ______________________ Date: ______________

Sorting materials

1

wood

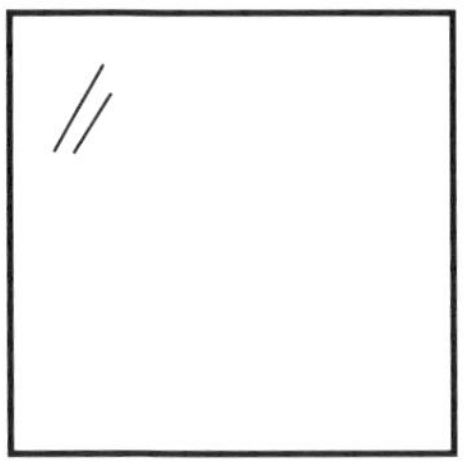

glass

a) One way wood and glass are the same is

_______________________________________ .

b) One way wood and glass are different is

_______________________________________ .

2 marks

2 Colour two materials that might be shiny.

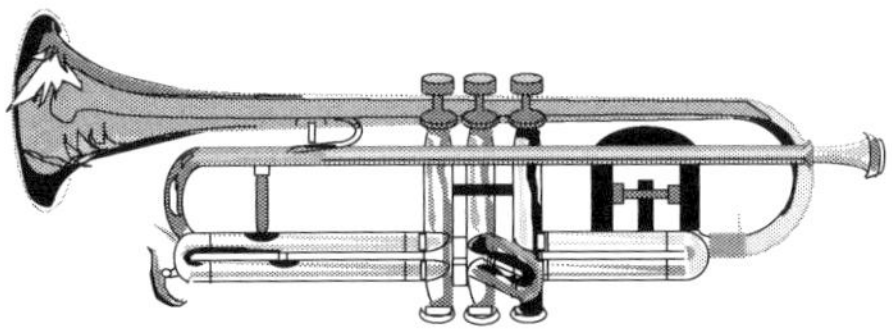

brass

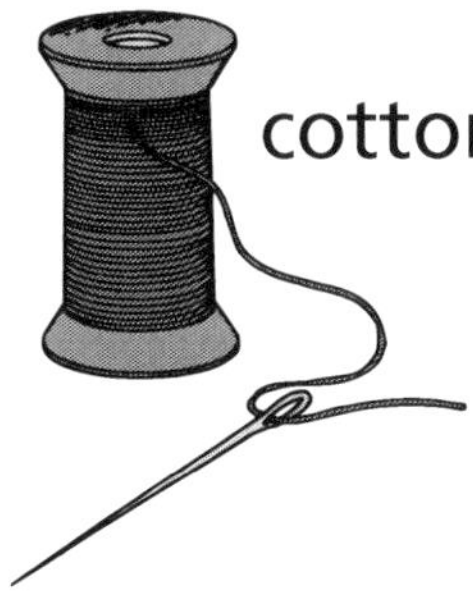

cotton

soil

diamond

2 marks

3 Write one more material in each group.

Soft	**Strong**
 butter	 steel
 wool	 wood

2 marks

Sorting materials

4 Name these groups. The first one has been done for you.

Materials which break easily

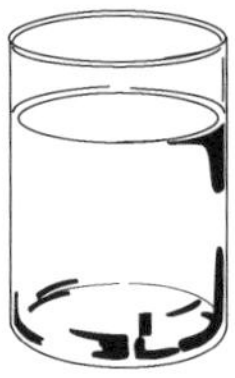

glass

pottery

china

Materials which ______________________________

glue

jam

mud

Materials which ______________________________

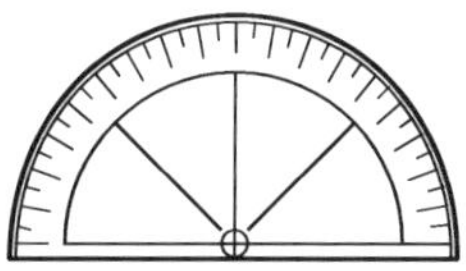

plastic

rubber

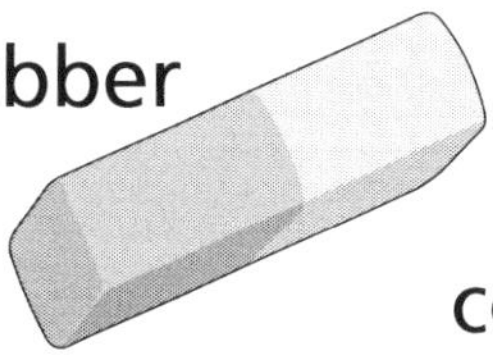

concrete

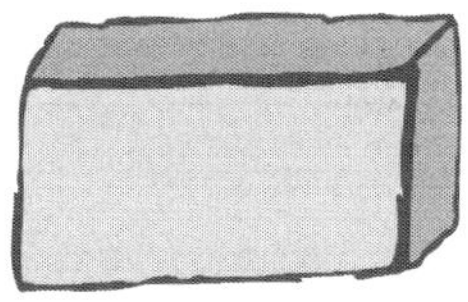

2 marks

5 Group these materials and name your groups.

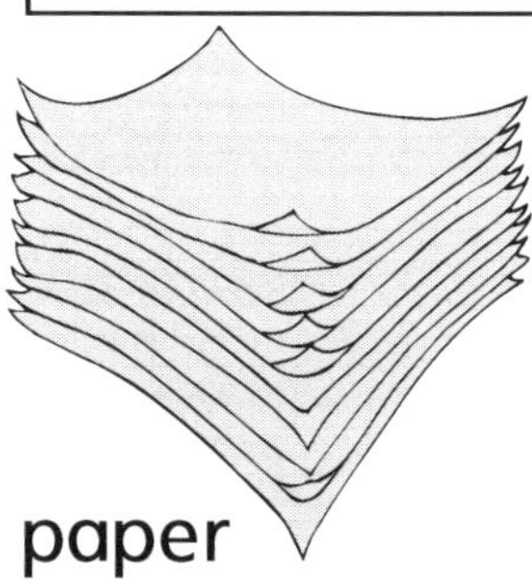

paper

chalk

fur

wool

2 marks

I can ______________________________

____

Total marks

Name: ____________________ Date: ____________________

Changing materials

4 marks

1 a) Declan squashes some materials with his hand. He lets go and checks to see if he has made a new shape. Circle the materials that keep their new shape.

clay

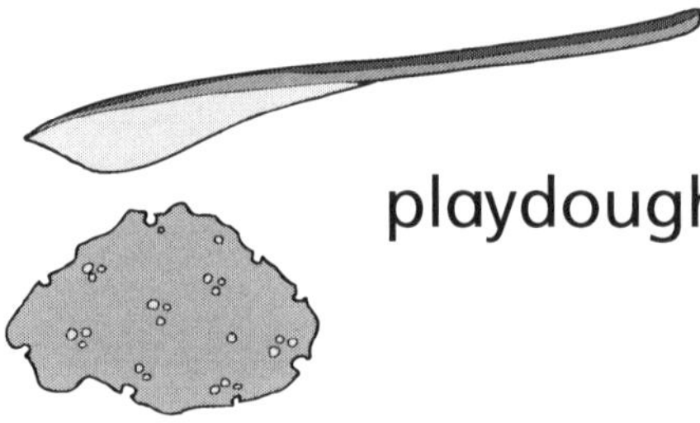

playdough

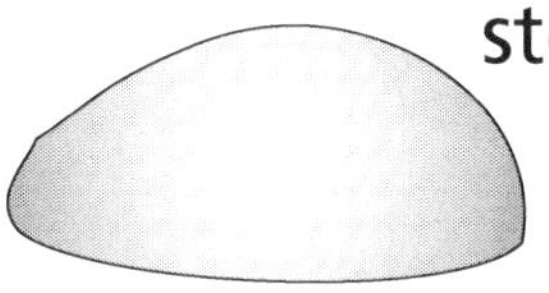

stone

bath sponge

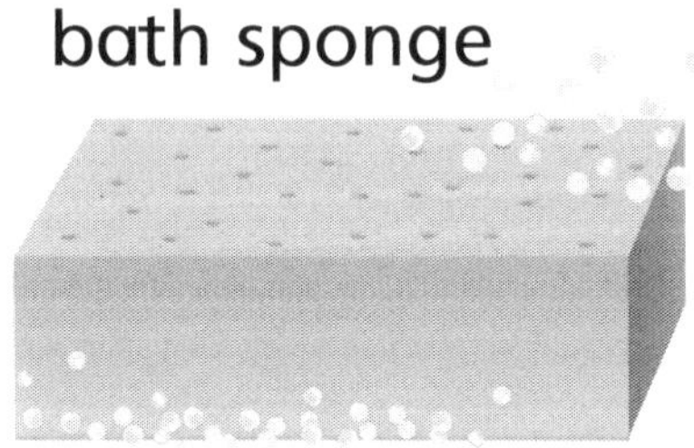

b) He stretches some materials. He lets go and checks to see if they have changed shape. Circle the materials that keep their new shape.

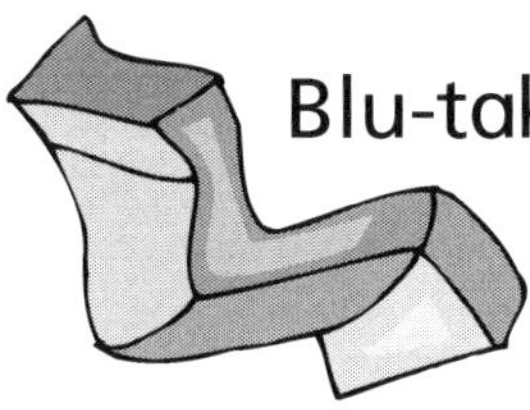

Blu-tak

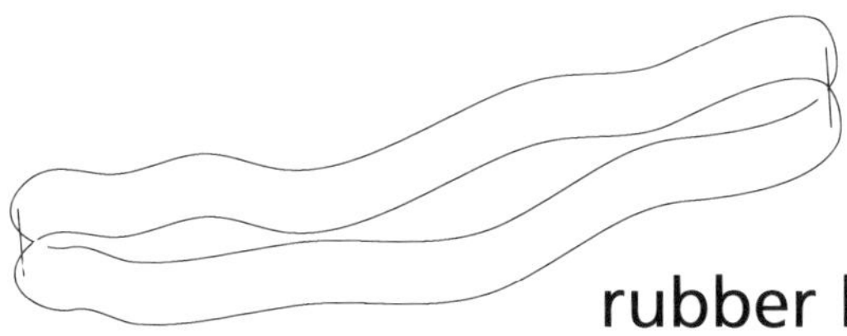

rubber band

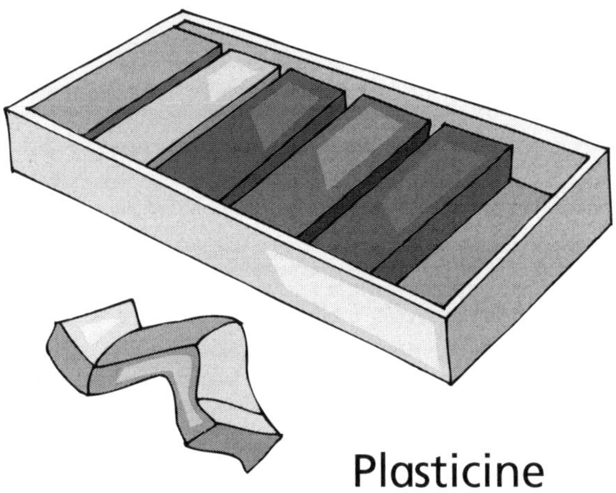

Plasticine

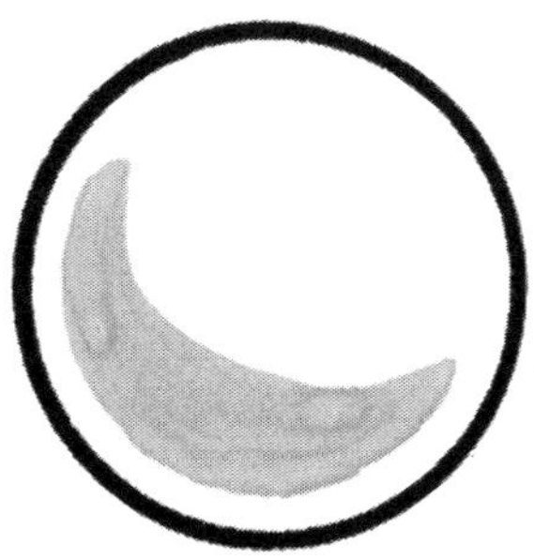

foam ball

Changing materials

2 Which materials will change when they are warmed in a pan?

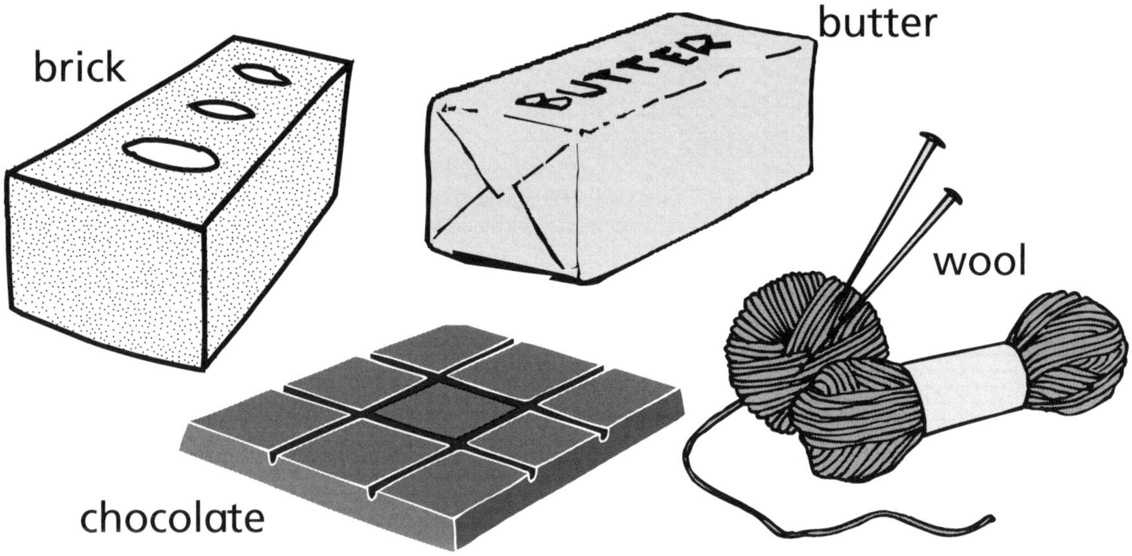

2 marks

3 Which materials will change when they are cooled in a freezer?

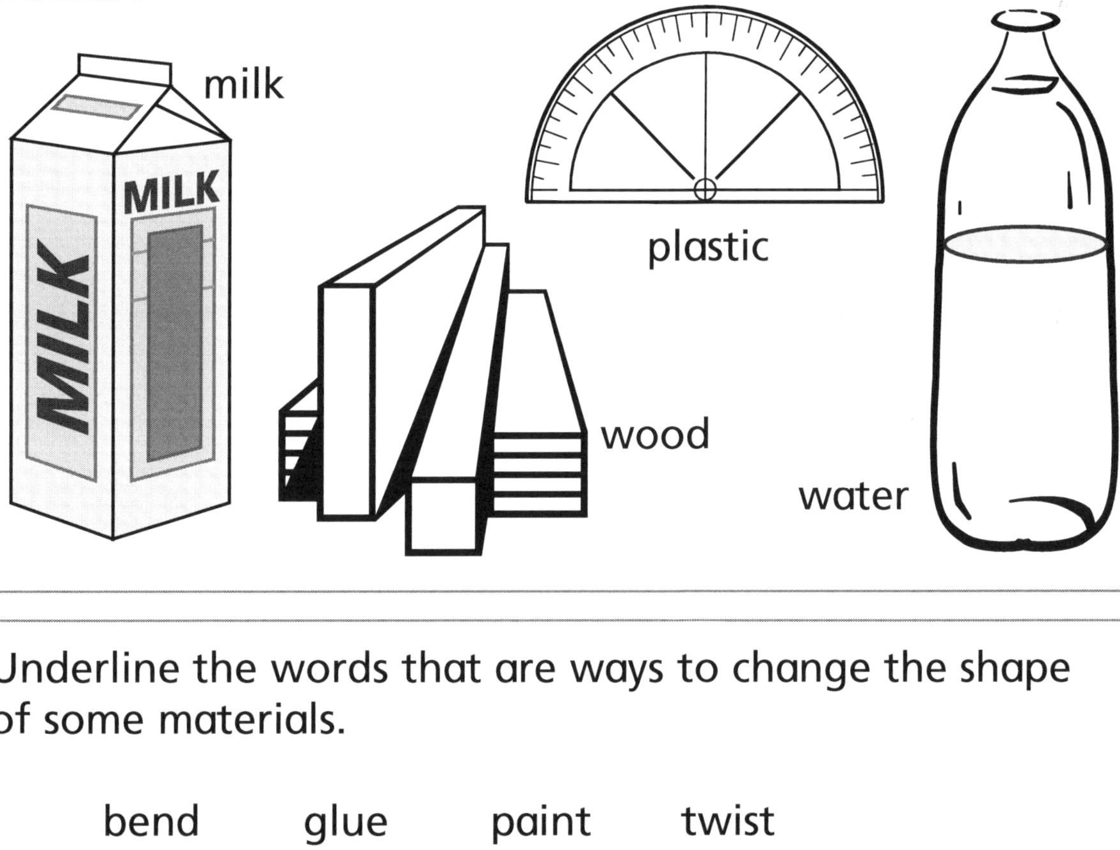

2 marks

4 Underline the words that are ways to change the shape of some materials.

bend glue paint twist

2 marks

I can ______________________________

____

Total marks

Name: ______________________ Date: ______________

Electricity

1 **a)** Draw and label something that makes sounds using electricity.

4 marks

b) Draw and label something that moves using electricity.

c) Draw and label something that makes light using electricity.

d) Draw and label something that makes heat using electricity.

Electricity

2 Join the labels to the parts of the circuit.

battery   bulb   switch   wires

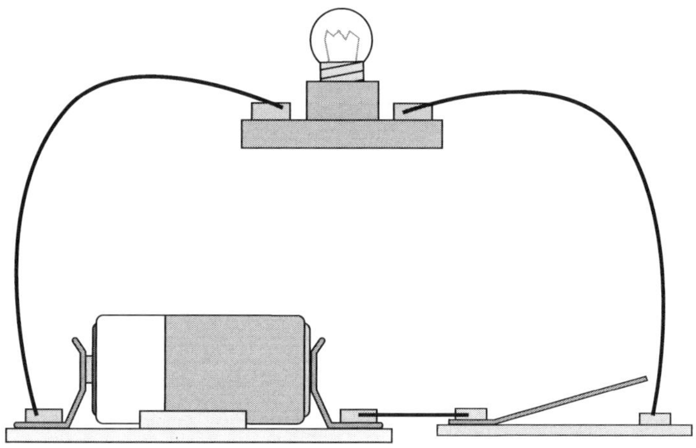

2 marks

3 **a)** Why are electrical sockets dangerous?

____

b) Why are batteries safer?

____

2 marks

4 **a)** Colour in blue the battery you would use in a watch.

b) Colour in red the battery you would use in a toy car.

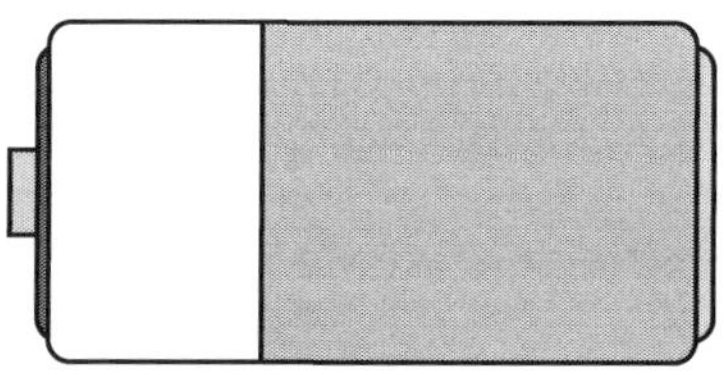

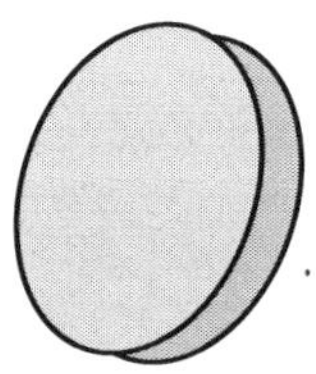

2 marks

I can ____

____

Total marks

Name: ______________________ Date: ______________

Sound

1 We hear sounds with our ______________.

1 mark

2 How do we make sounds on these instruments?

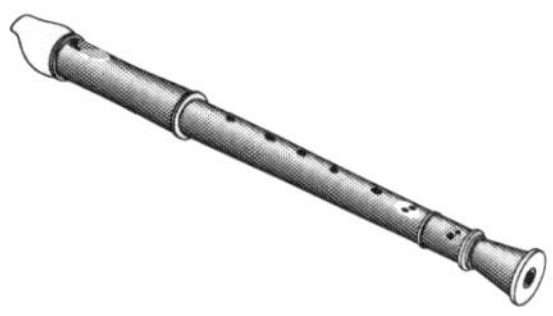

____

____

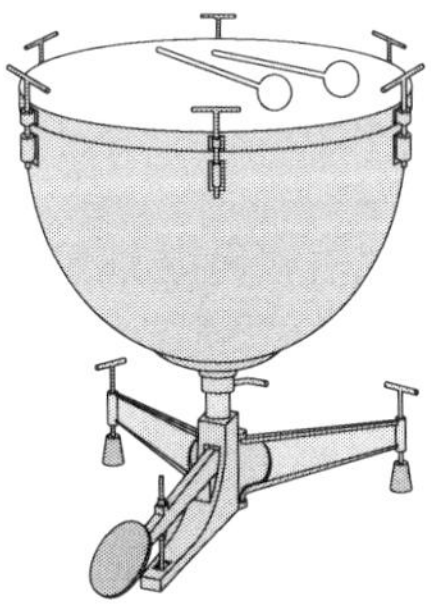

____

____

____

____

2 marks

3 Why can't Jack hear the teacher?

Jack

____

____

____

____

Teacher

2 marks

4 Choose words from the box to describe these sounds. Only use each word once.

loud	**soft**	**low**	**high**

a) a bird singing ____________

b) a lorry driving ____________

c) an aeroplane taking off ____________

d) a dog growling ____________

4 marks

5 Colour the one that makes the loudest sound.

motorbike

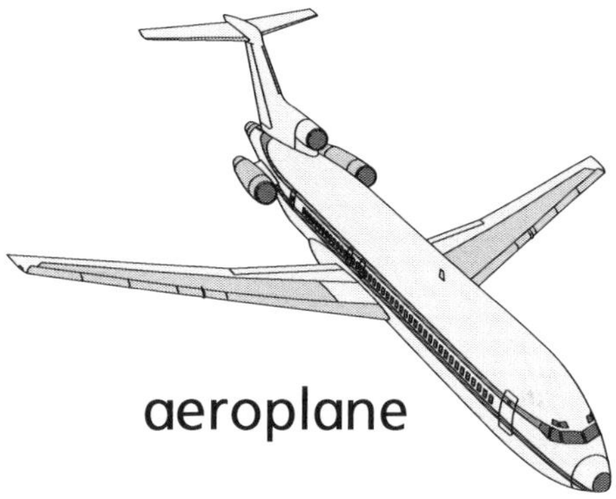

aeroplane

1 mark

6 Colour the animal that makes the highest sound.

cat

mouse

cow

1 mark

I can ____

____

Total marks

Name: ______________________ Date: ______________

Forces

1 Two children race across the playground. Colour the child who is going faster.

1 mark

2 Pushes and pulls are ____________________ .

1 mark

3 Write **push** or **pull** in the spaces.

a) Opening a drawer is a _____________ .

b) Switching a light on is a _____________ .

c) Pedalling a bike is a _____________ .

d) Stretching a rubber band is a _____________ .

4 marks

4 What makes the boat move?

____

____

____

1 mark

5 What makes the log move?

____

1 mark

6 What makes the car move?

____

1 mark

7 You can change the direction of the ball by

____

1 mark

I can ______________________________________

____

Total marks

Name: ______________________ Date: ______________

Light

1 Draw and label two sources of light.

2 marks

2 One night Pat looks around a dark room with a torch.

Later, Jim switches on the light to look around the room.

a) Who can see best? ______________________

b) Why? ______________________

____

2 marks

3 Circle the pictures that show where the necklace would be shiny.

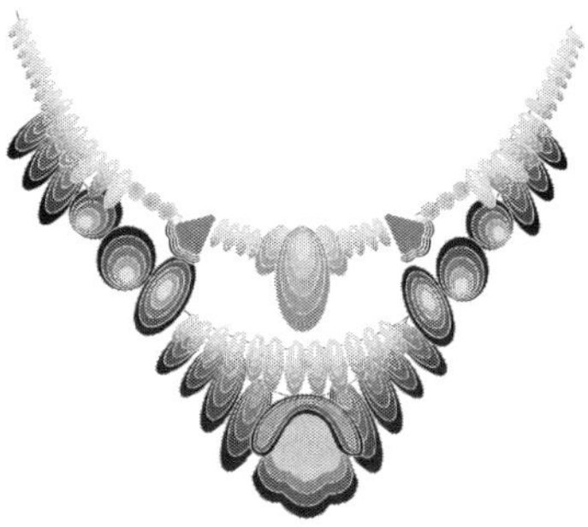

2 marks

4 What gives us most light? ______________________________

1 mark

5

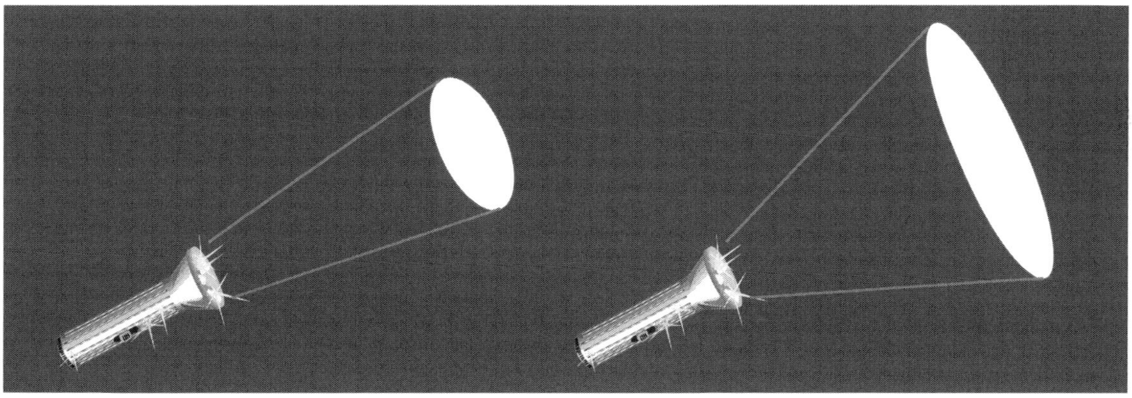

a) Circle the brightest torch.

b) How can you tell? ______________________________

____

2 marks

I can ______________________________

____

Total marks

Name: ____________________ Date: ____________

Activity B

1

a) Fill in the blank labels to show how the flowers were sorted.

2 marks

b) Lisa thought flowers always grew on the same stem as the leaves. Look at the flowers in the groups. Is she right?

____

1 mark

c) How can you tell?

____

____

1 mark

Sub-total

Activity B

2 Tick the places where a duck might live.

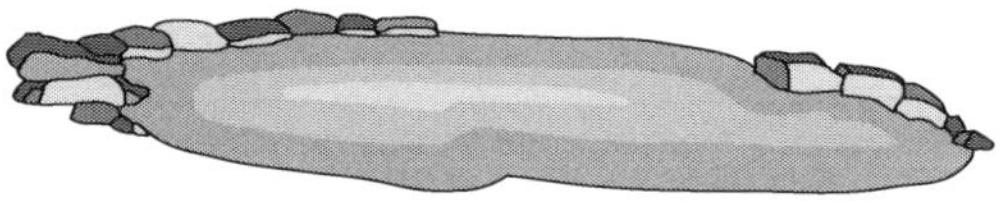

2 marks

3 Underline the **four** things that plants and animals need to stay alive.

food friends air light

home exercise water

2 marks

4 Tick the words that are what **all** living things do:

move run talk reproduce grow

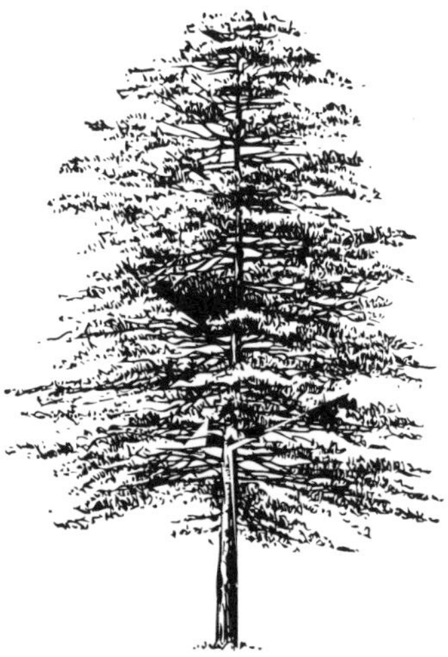

2 marks

Sub-total

Activity B

5 **a)** How does ice cream change as it warms up?

____

b) What happens to playdough if you stretch it?

____

2 marks

6 Complete the sentences.

*e.g. A material that is hard and strong is **stone**.*

a) A material that is bendy and strong is ____________ .

b) A material that is soft and strong is ____________ .

c) A material that is smooth and shiny is ____________ .

d) A material that is manmade and strong is

____________ .

4 marks

7 **a)** How are steel and stone the same?

____

b) How are steel and stone different?

____

2 marks

Sub-total

Activity B

8

a) The car alarm goes off. Circle the child who hears the softest sound.

b) Explain why they hear a softer sound.

____

c) The car lights are on. Why can't you tell?

____

d) When will the car lights look bright?

____

4 marks

9 Two cars set off from the start at the same time.

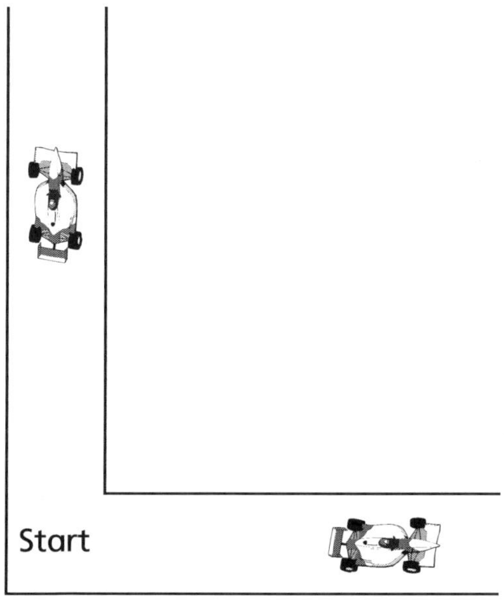

a) What is different about the way they are moving?

____

b) What is the same about the way they are moving?

____

2 marks

Sub-total

Activity B

10 Circle the animal that makes the loudest sound.

1 mark

Total marks

ACTIVITY A

1. labels correctly written
1 mark for two labels correctly written, 2 marks for all correctly written
2. owl, ladybird, fly
1 mark for two correct, 2 marks for all correct
3. two features of an elephant, e.g. it has a trunk, it has big ears, it is grey
1 mark each, up to 2 marks
4. two features of a rock, e.g. it is cold/hard/rough
1 mark each up to 2 marks
5. bulb will light/come on
'bulb' must be mentioned for the mark to be awarded
6. drawer will open
7. **a)** torch, Sun, streetlight and TV coloured
1 mark for three correct, 2 marks for all correct; deduct 1 mark for each incorrect answer
b) objects coloured correctly identified, even if incorrectly spelled
1 mark for two correct and 2 marks for all correct
8. push it/pull it/put it on a slope and let it go

ACTIVITY 1 COLLECTING DATA

1. **a)** wet soil circled
b) put them back where he found them/put them in a suitable habitat
2. **a)** Callum
b) Jill
c) Jill
3. **a)** Amy
b) reference to it being easier to compare or reference to different conditions on different days (e.g. they might be hungrier one day than the other)
1 mark for reasonable attempt at answer
c) put out milk and water and see which they drink most of
1 mark for some attempt at this

ACTIVITY 2 INTERPRETING RESULTS

1. **a)** no
b) candle doesn't need electricity
2. **a)** four
b) flowerbed and tree
1 mark for both
c) three
d) under a stone
e) 10
3. **a)** bell and drum circled
1 mark for both
b) wood block circled
c) no

ACTIVITY 3 LIVING THINGS

1. **a)** mushroom, plant and cat circled
1 mark for two correct, 2 marks for all correct; no marks if the doll is ticked
b) mushroom, plant and cat ticked
1 mark for two correct, 2 marks for all correct; no marks if the doll is ticked
2 **a)** fish, caterpillar and dog circled
1 mark for two correct, 2 marks for all correct; no marks if the flag or car is ticked
b) fish, caterpillar and dog ticked
1 mark for two correct, 2 marks for all correct; no marks if the flag or car is ticked
3. drawing of some food source for a rabbit (e.g. grass, carrots, any green plant)
4. water and food ticked
1 mark for both

ACTIVITY 4 GROUPING LIVING THINGS

1. drawing of two animals in 'No legs', e.g. worm, snake, snail; drawing of two animals in 'Four legs' (e.g. sheep, elephant)
   1 mark for two animals correct, 2 marks for all correct
2. two appropriate labels, e.g. cacti/no leaves; plants with flowers or desert/garden plants
3. 'can fly': bat, bird, fly; 'can't fly': frog, penguin, dog
   1 mark for two correct, 2 marks for all correct
4. drawing of one appropriate plant in each group (e.g. apple, potato, peas in first group; ivy, daffodils in second group)
   1 mark for each
5. various answers possible (e.g. four legs/not four legs; furry/not furry)
   1 mark for partially correct grouping, 2 marks for completely correct answers; accept any reasonable grouping

ACTIVITY 5 PLANTS

1. **a)** reference to the plant being bigger in some way (e.g. taller, more leaves)
   b) light, water and warmth
   1 mark for two correctly ticked, 2 marks for three correctly ticked; deduct 1 mark for each incorrect tick
2. labels written correctly
   1 mark for two labelled correctly, 2 marks for all labelled correctly
3. buttercup, dandelion, daffodil, daisy
   1 mark for two labelled correctly, 2 marks for all labelled correctly
4. reference to correct uses, e.g. food, shelter, clothing, decoration
   1 mark for each up to 2 marks
5. an apple tree

ACTIVITY 6 ANIMALS

1. cat – kitten; butterfly – caterpillar; chicken – chick
   1 mark for all correct
2. whiskers, fur, hoof/hooves and udders – two labels correctly filled in
   1 mark per label; 4 marks for all correct
3. insect, fish and human circled
   1 mark for two correct, 2 marks for three correct; deduct one mark for each incorrect circle
4. frog or toad (or a newt)
5. water and food
   1 mark each; deduct one mark for each incorrect circle
6. kangaroo, zebra, tiger, giraffe
   1 mark for two correct, 2 marks for all correct

ACTIVITY 7 HABITATS

1. fish – pond, slug – under a rock, mole – in the soil, squirrel – in a tree
   1 mark for two correct, 2 marks for all correct
2. each cross in a cool, damp place, e.g. in the stone wall, under the log
   1 mark each up to 2 marks
3. **a)** each pond-dwelling creature named correctly, e.g. fish, water snail
   1 mark each up to 2 marks
   b) each tree-dwelling creature named correctly, e.g. squirrel, bird
   1 mark each up to 2 marks
4. each difference identified, e.g. there is sand on the beach and soil in the forest; there is more water on the beach, there are trees in the forest and not on the beach
   1 mark each up to 2 marks

ACTIVITY 8 HUMANS

1. shoulder, forehead, elbow and ankle
   1 mark for three labels correct, 2 marks for all correct
2. **a)** two similarities correctly identified, e.g. all have faces/all have fingers/all have feelings/all bleed when cut
   b) one difference correctly identified, e.g. different colour hair/eyes/skin, different heights
3. an attribute that can't be changed correctly identified, e.g. your height/the size of your hand/foot
4. it will grow/be bigger/be stronger
5. reference to the fact that medicines can make you ill/kill you
6. for example hot, tired, sweaty, achy
   1 mark for each correct word up to 2 marks

ACTIVITY 9 PROPERTIES OF MATERIALS

1. brick and plastic coloured
   1 mark each up to 2 marks
2. **a)** suitable material for making a table, e.g. wood, plastic
   b) suitable material for making a coat, e.g. wool, leather
3. plastic and slate coloured
4. glass – transparent, wood – strong, rubber – bendy, wool – warm
   1 mark for two correct, 2 marks for all correct
5. each object named that could be made from metal, e.g. car, pan, watch, jewellery, washing machine, chair legs
   1 mark each up to 2 marks

ACTIVITY 10 SORTING MATERIALS

1. **a)** one similarity correctly identified, e.g. both rigid, solid
   b) one difference correctly identified, e.g. wood is strong, glass breaks easily; wood is opaque, glass is transparent (you can see through glass)
2. brass and diamond coloured
   1 mark each; deduct 1 mark for each material incorrectly coloured
3. one material correctly added to each set, e.g. soft – cotton, silk; strong – stone, brick
   1 mark each up to 2 marks
4. Second set: materials which are runny/sticky/wet or other appropriate attribute. Third set: materials which are manmade/long-lasting or other appropriate attribute
   1 mark for each up to 2 marks
5. materials correctly grouped and appropriately labelled, e.g. soft – wool, fur; used for writing – paper, chalk/manmade – paper; natural – wool, fur, chalk
   1 mark each for grouping and labelling, up to 2 marks

ACTIVITY 11 CHANGING MATERIALS

1. **a)** clay and playdough
   1 mark each up to 2 marks
   b) Blu-tak and Plasticine
   1 mark each up to 2 marks
2. butter and chocolate
   1 mark each, up to 2 marks
3. milk and water
   1 mark each up to 2 marks
4. bend and twist
   1 mark each up to 2 marks

ACTIVITY 12 ELECTRICITY

1. **a)** drawing and label of radio, TV, MP3 player, CD player, phone, etc.
   b) washing machine/toy car/fan/electric drill
   c) lamp/TV/computer/torch
   d) electric fire/cooker/kettle/iron
2. check labels are correctly joined
   1 mark for two correct, 2 marks for four correct
3. **a)** reference to high power (voltage) electricity killing/burning people; people can get electric shocks
   b) reference to the fact that they don't have much power (low voltage)
4. **a)** small round battery coloured blue
   b) AA battery coloured red

ACTIVITY 13 SOUND

1. ears
2. recorder – blow; drum – hit/bang/beat; guitar – pluck/strum
   1 mark for two correct, 2 marks for all correct
3. He's too far away/the teacher is too quiet
4. **a)** high/soft
   b) low/loud
   c) low/loud
   d) soft/low
   1 mark each; deduct 1 mark for each word used more than once
5. aeroplane coloured
6. mouse coloured

ACTIVITY 14 FORCES

1. colour the child in front
2. forces
3. **a)** pull
   b) push
   c) push
   d) pull
   1 mark each
4. the wind/air
5. the water
6. the engine
7. kicking/hitting it

ACTIVITY 15 LIGHT

1. drawing of two sources of light, e.g. Sun, electric light, torch, candle
   1 mark each
2. **a)** Jim
   b) reference to the fact that he has more light or it is brighter
3. sunny day and spotlighted area circled
   1 mark each (deduct one mark for each incorrect answer)
4. the Sun
5. **a)** second torch circled (with wider, longer beam)
   b) reference to the fact that you can see more or that it has a bigger beam or that the lit area/beam is wider

ACTIVITY B

1. **a)** first set labelled with reference to long, straight leaves; second set labelled with reference to round, bumpy-edged leaves
   1 mark for each set labelled in an appropriate way, up to 2 marks
   b) No
   c) some of the flowers have their own stems
2. pond and river
   1 mark each; deduct 1 mark for each incorrect answer
3. food, air, light and water
   1 mark for three correct and one incorrect; 2 marks for all correct; deduct 1 mark for each incorrect answer
4. reproduce and grow
5. **a)** it melts/goes runny/changes to a liquid
   b) it changes shape/gets longer/gets thinner
6. **a)** e.g. rubber
   b) e.g. leather
   c) e.g. silver
   d) e.g. concrete
7. **a)** e.g. they are hard/strong/both solids
   b) steel can be bent, stone can't/steel is manmade, stone is natural
8. **a)** circle child furthest from car
   b) because they are further away
   c) because the Sun is shining/it is light
   d) at night/in the dark
9. **a)** different directions
   b) same speed/distance
10. lion circled